In the Begin

On the first day God c
Genesis 1:3-5

M000188131

Color the picture.

Day 2

On the second day God separated the waters
so that there was sky above and water on the land.
Genesis 1:6-8

Use all your blue pencils to color this picture.

Day 3

On the third day dry land appeared and plants started to grow.
Genesis 1:9-13

Color the picture and add some flowers and trees.

Day 4

On the fourth day God made the sun, moon and stars.
Genesis 1:14-19

Color the picture and add some stars.

Day 5

On the fifth day God made the fish in the sea and the birds in the air.
Genesis 1:20-23

Color the picture and count the
fish and birds.

Day 6

On the sixth day God made animals and the first people,
Adam and Eve. On the seventh day God rested.
Genesis 1:24-2:3

Color the picture and name the animals.

Spot the Difference

God created our wonderful world in six days!
Just look around and thank Him for the amazing animals
and beautiful plants and flowers that you can see!

Spot 5 differences in the pictures below.

The earth is the LORD's,
and everything in it. The world
and all its people belong to Him.
Psalm 24:1

Animal Antics

The Garden of Eden must have been filled with all kinds of wonderful animals – big, small, hairy, smooth, loud and quiet!

Count to see how many animals there are in this picture. Then you can color them all in.

In the beginning God created the heavens and the earth. Genesis 1:1

Farm Animal Fun

Can you make the sounds of all these farm animals?
Fill in their names to complete the crossword puzzle.

Cat

Cow

Rooster

Chicken

Dog

Sheep

Duck

Goat

Pig

Horse

Turkey

Shout to the Lord, all the earth;
break out in praise and sing for joy!
Psalm 98:4

Bible Animal Shadow Match

All of these animals are mentioned in the Bible.
Match the animal to its shadow. See if you can think of
where in the Bible these animals are mentioned.

The godly care for their animals. Proverbs 12:10

Little Lamb Dot-to-Dot

Do you know that you are God's precious little lamb?
He loves you and cares for you very much.

Join the dots and color the picture of these cute lambs.

**He tends His flock like a shepherd: He gathers the lambs in His arms
and carries them close to His heart; He gently leads those that have young.**
Isaiah 40:11

Burning Bush Maze

God spoke to Moses from the burning bush. He had a very important job for Moses. Moses obeyed God and saved the Israelites from being slaves in Egypt.

The angel of the LORD appeared to Moses in a blazing fire from the middle of a bush. Moses stared in amazement. Though the bush was engulfed in flames, it didn't burn up.

Exodus 3:2

Sheep Shadow Match

David looked after sheep when he was young.
He made sure they were safe and had enough food and water.
David looked after his sheep just like God looks after us.

Match the sheep to its shadow.

The LORD is my shepherd; I have all that I need. Psalm 23:1

Helpful Rebekah

Abraham was looking for a wife for Isaac. He sent his servant to find a wife. When the servant met Rebekah and she kindly gave him and his camels water, he knew that she was the right girl for Isaac.

Spot 12 differences between the pictures

When Rebekah had given him a drink, she said, "I'll draw water for your camels, too, until they have had enough to drink." So she quickly emptied her jug into the watering trough and ran back to the well to draw water for all his camels.

Genesis 24:19-20

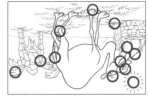

Strong Samson

Samson was given tremendous strength by God.
He defeated the Philistines with his great strength.

Join the dots and color the picture.

God arms me
with strength,
and He makes
my way
perfect.
Psalm 18:32

Daniel in the Lions' Den

Daniel obeyed God and prayed to God even when the law said he was not allowed to. Daniel was thrown into a den of lions, but God protected him and kept him safe!

Join the dots and color the picture.

"My God sent His angel to shut the lions' mouths so that they would not hurt me, for I have been found innocent in His sight." Daniel 6:22

A Whale of a Time!

Jonah disobeyed God when He told him to go to Nineveh and preach to the people. Jonah was swallowed by a big fish that spat him out 3 days later. Inside the fish's belly Jonah prayed and asked God to forgive him. Then he went straight to Nineveh as God had told him to.

Join the dots and add some fish in the sea and birds in the sky.

This time Jonah obeyed the LORD's command and went to Nineveh. Jonah 3:3

Bible Character Match

God spoke to Noah, Daniel and Moses and told them what He wanted them to do. When God tells us to do something we must obey Him straightaway.

Link these Bible characters to the correct image.

Jesus replied, "Anyone who loves Me will obey My teaching." John 14:23

No Room in the Inn

Mary and Joseph had to stay in a stable when they arrived in Bethlehem because there was no room anywhere else. Baby Jesus was born in the stable that night and laid in a manger.

Help Mary and Joseph to reach the stable.

Mary gave birth to her firstborn Son. She wrapped Him snugly in strips of cloth and laid Him in a manger, because there was no lodging available for them.

Luke 2:7

Spot the Difference

Baby Jesus was born in a stable where farm animals stayed. His bed was a manger, which was where the animals ate their hay. It is amazing to think that God's Son, the King of kings, was born in such a humble place.

Spot 10 differences between the pictures.

The angel said to Joseph, "Mary will have a Son, and you are to name Him Jesus, for He will save His people from their sins."
Matthew 1:21

The Way of the Wise Men

The wise men came from the east and followed the special star that led them to Baby Jesus. They gave gifts of gold, frankincense and myrrh to Jesus.

Help the wise men to reach Mary, Joseph and Baby Jesus so that they can give Him their gifts.

Little Donkey Dot-to-Dot

Donkeys are very humble and hardworking animals.
Jesus rode into Jerusalem on a colt, which is a young donkey.
The donkey had never been ridden before.

Join the dots and color in this donkey.

They brought the colt to Jesus and threw their garments over it for Him to ride on. As He rode along, the crowds spread out their garments on the road ahead of Him. Luke 19:35-36

Children Are Special to Jesus

Jesus always made time for children.
Count how many children you can see in this picture.

Children, always obey your parents,
for this pleases the Lord. Colossians 3:20

Four Friends with Great Faith

There were four friends who had a friend who couldn't walk. They knew Jesus could heal him so they lowered their friend down to Jesus from the roof of the house where Jesus was. Jesus saw the men's faith and healed their friend!

Help the men to get their friend to Jesus.

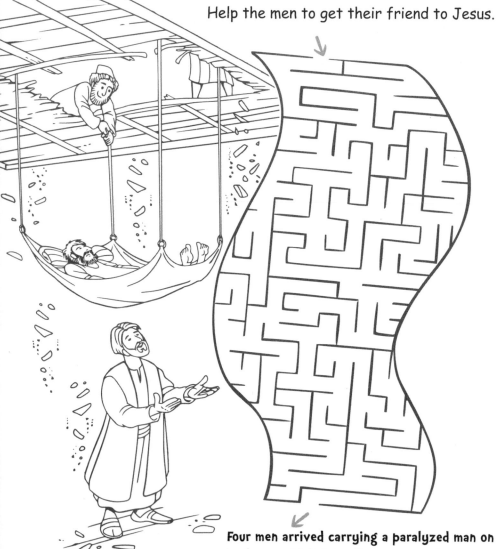

Four men arrived carrying a paralyzed man on a mat. They couldn't bring him to Jesus because of the crowd, so they dug a hole through the roof above His head. Then they lowered the man on his mat, right down in front of Jesus. Seeing their faith, Jesus said to the paralyzed man, "My child, your sins are forgiven." Mark 2:3-5

Zacchaeus Meets Jesus

Help Zacchaeus to climb down the sycamore tree and meet Jesus.

When Jesus came by, He looked up at Zacchaeus and called him by name. "Zacchaeus!" He said. "Quick, come down! I must be a guest in your home today." Zacchaeus quickly climbed down and took Jesus to his house in great excitement and joy. Luke 19:5-6

Fruit of the Spirit

Find the 9 fruits of the Spirit in the word search below. These are the qualities God wants us to have in our lives.

Love
Joy
Peace
Patience
Kindness
Goodness
Faithfulness
Gentleness
Self-control

F	R	B	E	S	G	K	G	U	A	P	O	A	N	A
O	Z	I	M	N	S	E	X	O	C	U	K	L	W	B
L	K	J	H	A	E	S	N	Y	O	J	C	I	U	F
A	L	Y	L	O	V	E	S	T	A	D	E	X	Q	X
X	O	A	A	T	W	L	R	T	L	A	N	A	W	A
L	M	C	B	U	Q	F	U	A	L	E	Y	E	Z	Q
P	A	T	I	E	N	C	E	I	A	H	N	B	S	V
P	K	P	Y	E	W	O	C	N	P	M	K	E	T	S
Q	X	R	Y	K	I	N	D	N	E	S	S	I	S	U
F	G	R	N	E	S	T	Y	I	A	I	F	G	A	S
T	J	W	O	I	A	R	Q	L	C	K	A	R	Y	A
H	O	J	M	U	K	O	X	H	E	G	E	N	J	I
B	A	O	W	D	S	L	F	R	A	L	K	H	T	S
S	S	Y	K	W	H	Z	C	O	K	F	D	E	V	G
A	K	U	F	A	I	T	H	F	U	L	N	E	S	S

The Holy Spirit produces this kind of fruit in our lives: love, joy, peace, patience, kindness, goodness, faithfulness, gentleness, and self-control. There is no law against these things! Galatians 5:22-23

Alphabet Jumble

A, B, C ... Jesus loves me!

See if you can spot and color all the letters of the alphabet. Use the block below to write something that you are thankful to God for.

I am grateful for _____

_____

Bloom Where God Plants You!

1	2	3	4	5	6	7
Yellow	Orange	Green	Red	Purple	Blue	Pink

The grass withers and the flowers fade, but the word of our God stands forever.

Isaiah 40:8

Angel Dot-to-Dot

The angels in heaven worship God for His greatness and power.
Angels are also God's messengers on earth.

Join the dots and color the angel.

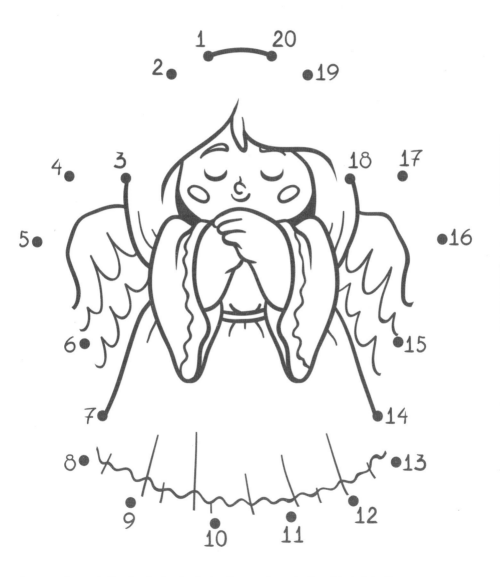

The angels said, "Holy, holy, holy is the Lord God, the Almighty." Revelation 4:8

Jesus Loves the Little Children!

Did you know that Jesus loves children, just like you? Children all over the world are precious to Him.

Color the picture and write your name on the line below.

Jesus loves _____

Jesus said, "Let the children come to Me. Don't stop them! For the Kingdom of Heaven belongs to those who are like these children." Matthew 19:14

The Armor of God

Color in the picture then cut out the pieces of armor and stick them on the boy.

Put on the armor of God:

1. the belt of truth
2. the breastplate of God's righteousness
3. for shoes, put on the peace that comes from the Good News
4. hold up the shield of faith
5. put on salvation as your helmet
6. hold the sword of the Spirit, which is the word of God. (Ephesians 6:13-17)

Copyright © 2017 by Christian Art Kids, an imprint of Christian Art Publishers

First edition © 2017
Second edition © 2019

Scripture quotations are taken from the *Holy Bible*, New Living Translation, copyright © 1996, 2004, 2007, 2013, 2015 by Tyndale House Foundation. Used by permission of Tyndale House Publishers, Carol Stream, Illinois 60188. All rights reserved.

Images used under license from Shutterstock.com

Printed in China

ISBN 978-1-4321-3110-4

© All rights reserved. No part of this book may be reproduced in any form without permission in writing from the publisher, except in the case of brief quotations in critical articles or reviews.

22   23   24   25   26   27   28   29   30   31   –   14   13   12   11   10   9   8   7   6   5

Printed in Shenzhen, China
MARCH 2022
Print Run: PUR402284